DONALD
TRUMP

DONALD TRUMP

OUTSPOKEN PERSONALITY AND PRESIDENT

Jill Sherman

LERNER PUBLICATIONS ◆ MINNEAPOLIS

Lerner Publications Company
A division of Lerner Publishing Group, Inc.
241 First Avenue North
Minneapolis, MN USA 55401

For reading levels and more information, look up this title at www.lernerbooks.com.

The images in this book are used with the permission of: © Bastiaan Slabbers/Alamy, p. 2; © Ethan Miller/Getty Images, p. 6; Anthony Behar/Sipa via AP Images, pp. 8, 9; Wikimedia Commons, pp. 10, 21; © Jack Smith/NY Daily News Archive/Getty Images, p. 11; Seth Poppel Yearbook Library, p. 12; © Matthew Marcucci/Wikimedia Commons, p. 13; © Barton Silverman/ The New York Times/Redux, p. 14; © New York Daily News Archive/Getty Images, p. 16; © Don Hogan Charles/The New York Times/Redux, p. 17; © age fotostock/Alamy, p. 18; AP Photo, p. 19; © Christian Mueller/Shutterstock.com, p. 20; Library of Congress (HABS NJ-1130-1), p. 22; © Andre Jenny/Alamy, p. 24; © Ted Thai/The LIFE Images Collection/Getty Images, p. 25; AP Photo/Mike Derer, p. 26; AP Photo/Marty Lederhandler, p. 27; © Rose Hartman/Getty Images, p. 28; © ZUMA Press, Inc/Alamy, pp. 29, 30; AP Photo/Chris Pizzello, p. 31; AP Photo/Frank Franklin II, p. 33; © REUTERS/Alamy, p. 35; Polaris/Newscom, p. 37; © epa european pressphoto agency b.v./Alamy, p. 38; AP Photo/Richard Drew, p. 40; © Mark Wilson/Getty Images, p. 41.

Front cover: © Ethan Miller/Getty Images.

Main body text set in Rotis Serif Std 55 Regular 13.5/17. Typeface provided by Adobe Systems.

Library of Congress Cataloging-in-Publication Data

Names: Sherman, Jill, author.
Title: Donald Trump : outspoken personality and president / Jill Sherman.
Description: Minneapolis : Lerner Publications, [2017] | Includes bibliographical references and index.
Identifiers: LCCN 2016041485 (print) | LCCN 2016042154 (ebook) | ISBN 9781512425963 (library bound : alkaline paper) | ISBN 9781512427998 (eb pdf)
Subjects: Presidential candidates—United States—Biography—Juvenile literature.
Classification: LCC E887.C55 S477 2017 (print) | LCC E887.C55 (ebook) | DDC 973.932092 [B] —dc23

LC record available at https://lccn.loc.gov/2016041485

Manufactured in the United States of America
2-44139-23308-4/27/2017

CONTENTS

Donald Trump gives a thumbs-up after speaking at a campaign event.

On a sunny afternoon in June 2015, Donald J. Trump called a press conference in the lobby of Trump Tower. All the major media outlets had gathered, eager to know what the outspoken businessman and entertainer planned to say. Trump appeared with his wife, Melania, and the couple slowly descended an escalator amid flashing cameras and applause from those waiting to hear him speak.

Taking the podium, Trump grinned confidently. He spoke off the cuff, not reading from a prepared speech. He told the crowd that he thought American leaders needed to do more to make America great. He said that some leaders and policies were not helping the country the way they should. He said that America needed a new leader. Then he made an announcement: "So ladies and gentlemen, I am officially running for president of the United States, and we are going to make our country great again."

The announcement took the media by storm. Trump had been publicly talking about politics for some time.

Trump announced that he would run for president during a press conference at Trump Tower in June 2015.

Some had guessed that he might be planning to run for the presidency, but many doubted that he would seriously pursue the position.

But Trump was serious indeed. He went on to run a campaign like none that had ever been seen before. Instead of raising money as most candidates do, Trump funded most of his own campaign. More than any other candidate, he used Twitter to state his opinions and speak directly to the public. Unlike most other candidates, he did not have a background as a politician. Instead, Trump had experience in business and television. And he did not shy away from controversy. When Trump was criticized by other candidates and the media, he did not

Members of the press gathered in Trump Tower to listen to Trump speak and announce his run for political office.

back down. He made bold and controversial statements about the economy and about immigration. But the controversy did not seem to hurt his campaign. Instead, Trump roused support across the country.

Trump's status as a political outsider won voters over. Trump promised to lower taxes, keep jobs in the United States, and stop illegal immigration. And many Americans believed that Trump, more than more typical politicians, would take control and, as his campaign slogan stated, "make America great again."

Trump's supporters turned out in large numbers at the polls. And in November 2016, Trump won the election to become president of the United States. After a lifetime of striving to win, to be noticed, and to succeed, Trump gained one more incredible success as he won one of the most important and recognizable positions in the world.

WINNING INSTINCT

Trump's family had a history of being very successful. His grandfather, Friedrich Drumpf, immigrated to the United States in 1885. Like many immigrants, he changed his name to a more American spelling: Trump. In 1891 Friedrich Trump moved to Seattle, Washington, and opened a successful restaurant. When the Klondike gold rush (1896–1899) began in the Yukon Territory in northwestern Canada, he moved his business north to cater to those mining for gold. He opened the New Arctic Restaurant and Hotel in British Columbia in 1898. He also opened a restaurant in Whitehorse, Yukon. When the gold rush ended, Friedrich Trump sold the hotel and returned to New York as a wealthy man.

Trump's grandfather, Friedrich Trump, soon after immigrating to the United States

With this fortune, Fred Trump, Donald Trump's father, built his own business. As a builder and real estate developer, Fred Trump owned apartments in Queens, Staten Island, and Brooklyn, New York. He worked hard

Donald's father, Fred Trump, after buying an amusement park in Brooklyn, New York

and built a mansion home in Queens where he raised his family. Donald was born on June 14, 1946. He was the fourth of five children in the family. Fred Trump taught his children to be fiercely ambitious and to work hard. He required all of his children to work for their own money. Donald and his brothers, Robert and Fred Jr., had paper routes. Fred Trump was demanding of his children, but he also pampered them. When it rained or snowed, he allowed his sons to deliver their newspapers from a chauffeured limousine. He insisted that they were destined for greatness, and he often told Donald, "You are a king."

Donald, along with the other Trump children, attended the private Kew–Forest School. But at school, Donald was a troublemaker. He argued and got into fights with other students and teachers. By the time Donald reached eighth grade, Fred Trump saw that something had to change. He took Donald out of private school and sent him to New York Military Academy (NYMA) in 1959.

NYMA was an all-boys military school. It was located north of the city along the Hudson River, so Donald was separated from his family. He learned about discipline and respect. He was required to wear a uniform. And rules were strictly enforced.

At NYMA Donald also played football, baseball, and soccer. Donald's baseball coach told the team that

Donald (*center*) poses with other NYMA sports team captains for a yearbook photo in 1964.

winning was the only thing that mattered. A local newspaper highlighted Trump's athletic achievement with the headline "Trump Wins Game for NYMA." It was the first time Donald saw his name in print. This small taste of fame was thrilling. Donald knew that he wanted more.

Donald took after his father and showed a great interest in the family business. He would visit his father on job sites and watch the way he worked. As he watched, Donald picked up on his father's way of doing business. Fred Trump pressed his employees for the best work. He negotiated for better prices and faster schedules. He worked constantly, and Donald understood that this hard work and ability to make deals were the keys to his success.

After he graduated from NYMA, Donald attended Fordham University in the Bronx. He studied business, and since he knew he would later be involved in the family business, he spent most of his free time and weekends working with his father.

After two years at Fordham, Trump transferred to the more prestigious Wharton School. It is part of the

Cohen Hall at the University of Pennsylvania was once home to the Wharton School.

University of Pennsylvania, an Ivy League school. There, he absorbed all he could from his professors. He showed particular interest in learning about finance. In 1968 Trump graduated with a degree in economics.

MAKING CONNECTIONS

After graduation, Trump went to work for his father's company. Trump worked in his father's modest office in Brooklyn, but he dreamed of doing more. In December 1972, a potential client came to visit the Trump offices. Trump sold the client a property and, at the age of

Donald Trump and his father stand at a property in Brooklyn in 1973. Trump was an apprentice to his father at the time.

twenty-six, sealed his first multimillion-dollar deal.

This success helped Trump to expand the business. His father's business had focused on properties in Brooklyn, Queens, and Staten Island, New York. But Trump had his eye on Manhattan, an area of New York that is well known for high-profile people and businesses. He made connections with people in Manhattan. He knew this was the path to success. Trump explained, "The business is, yes, about putting up buildings, but it's also about dealing with these people. It's about being friendly with politicians. It's about having them respect you. It's about having them like you." Trump learned early on how to work with people to get ahead.

Trump also began to examine properties in Manhattan, looking for their unseen potential. In 1970 Penn Central Railroad had gone bankrupt. The company was selling the properties it owned. Trump and other developers were eager to buy these properties.

Trump made a deal for rail yard properties on Manhattan's West Side along the Hudson River. The area, known as Hell's Kitchen, was mostly undeveloped. It was full of warehouses and low-rent apartments. Crime was common. But Trump was drawn to the site. He saw possibilities for his company.

At first, Trump had planned to turn these properties into apartment complexes. But then he found out that the New York City government was searching for a site for a new convention center. So Trump promoted the properties

Trump (*left*) and New York's economic development administrator, Alfred Eisenpreis, look at a sketch of the renovation to the Commodore.

as a location for the city convention center. The city selected Trump's site in 1978.

Another Penn Central property, a hotel known as the Commodore, was next to Grand Central Station. Trump knew that this was a great location for a hotel. So he made a deal with Hyatt Hotels Corporation in 1975. Trump knew that Hyatt did not have a large hotel in that area. And he knew that he would be able to save money on development because the city was offering lower taxes on the property. He made a complex deal to upgrade the Commodore into a luxury hotel.

BUILDING AN EMPIRE

Trump quickly became president of the Trump Organization, and he began making a name for himself. He surrounded himself with the rich and powerful people of New York and soon met Czech-born fashion model Ivana Zelnickova. The two dated for about a year. Trump took her skiing in Aspen and introduced her to his parents in New York. On New Year's Eve, Trump proposed. The two married just four months later in April 1977.

The couple soon became a powerful team. Their relationship became highly public and so did their lavish lifestyle. Trump brought her into the Trump Organization as vice president of interior design. In this position, she took charge of the renovations of the Commodore Hotel. The outside of the hotel was designed by an architect named Der Scutt. He gave the building a modern look

Architect Der Scutt in his office in New York in 1997

17

Trump's Grand Hyatt Hotel (*left*) stands near New York City's iconic Chrysler Building.

with gleaming, reflective glass. It was a style that Trump found impressive and that he would use again in his future projects. When the hotel opened as the Grand Hyatt in 1980, it was an instant success.

Meanwhile, as the Commodore project was under way, Trump was working on another ambitious deal on a property on Fifth Avenue, a major street in Manhattan filled with famous and expensive shops. Trump negotiated to build a luxury tower near the iconic Tiffany jewelry store. But he first needed to get permission to build there. He asked Scutt to help him. As part of the negotiation, Trump asked Scutt to sketch a terribly ugly building. He presented this drawing at the start of the negotiations. Trump knew nobody would like the design. But he would seem flexible when he changed the design to something more artful—and to the way he actually wanted it.

The construction on the tower did not come without its problems. Trump demolished a historic building, which stood on his new tower's site. The building was known for two limestone sculptures that decorated the outside. The sculptures were valued at $200,000 each. Scutt hoped to keep the sculptures and use them in the new tower's lobby. Trump wanted something more modern, but he knew the statues were valuable. Rather

Trump demolished the historic Bonwit Teller department store to build his new tower on Fifth Avenue.

than using the statues in his tower, Trump promised to donate them to the Metropolitan Museum of Art. However, removing the art was more difficult and expensive than Trump had planned for. After costly delays, Trump decided they would have to demolish the art.

As the tower went up, Trump tried to save money on building the apartments and shops inside. But he made sure that the public areas of the building would be impressive. The completed fifty-eight-story tower opened in 1983. It featured a five-story atrium lined in pink marble, and it contained a 60-foot waterfall. The building was named Trump Tower.

The high-profile tower included luxury stores, offices, and apartments. Celebrities lived in the tower, which helped solidify Trump Tower's high-class image. Some of the apartments sold for as much as $10 million. Pop star Michael Jackson, movie director Steven Spielberg, and entertainer Johnny Carson all purchased homes in Trump's prestigious building. And with his name gleaming across the building's exterior, Trump himself was tied to the tower's elite.

Trump Tower in New York City

THE TRUMP ORGANIZATION

Donald Trump became the head of the Trump Organization, an international business headquartered at Trump Tower in New York, in the 1970s. His grandmother started the business in 1923 with her son (Donald Trump's father) Fred Trump. The business was originally named Elizabeth Trump & Son. When Donald Trump took over the business, he changed its name. The Trump Organization has varied businesses, particularly real estate, hotels, and golf courses. Retail, entertainment, publications, and marketing are also included in the Trump Organization. Trump's oldest three children, Donald Jr., Ivanka, and Eric, all came to hold key roles in the Trump Organization and took over its operation as their father became increasingly involved in politics.

Trump's grandmother, Elizabeth Trump

TRUMP GAMBLES ON ATLANTIC CITY

While continuing to develop properties in New York, Trump saw a new business opportunity in nearby New Jersey. In 1976 voters had approved gambling in the seaside tourist destination of Atlantic City. The flashy, glamorous lifestyle and the large sums of money flowing in and out of casinos drew Trump's interest. As Trump put it, "To me a gambler is someone who plays the slot machines. I prefer to own slot machines. It's very good business being the house." In other words, Trump wanted to be part of the casino business.

Trump quickly began negotiating a lease for an excellent property near the Atlantic City Convention Hall. He also worked to get the licenses he would need to

Trump would eventually own a casino near the Atlantic City Convention Hall, shown here.

operate a casino. But this new venture was more difficult than Trump had expected. In New York, Trump had strong business relationships with other developers and city officials. But he did not have as many connections in Atlantic City. And although gambling had been legalized, many people in Atlantic City still viewed it as a shady business. Few were eager to get into business with Trump.

But the hotel company Holiday Inn knew about Trump's desire to develop properties in Atlantic City. They approached him with a deal. Holiday Inn wanted the property near the convention center for their Harrah's casino-hotel. So Holiday Inn offered to invest $50 million in construction on the property, and they would manage the casino once it was built. After the new casino-hotel was up and running, Holiday Inn would split the profits with Trump.

As construction neared completion, Trump brought his wife in to design the interiors. As with the Commodore, the Trumps wanted to attract high-class clients to the casino. So she gave the casino a high-end, dazzling look. However, the Trumps' vision did not match Harrah's. The casino managers wanted to draw a large crowd of people regardless of their income level. They were angry that Trump had not built a parking garage for clients who drove in from out of town. Harrah's at Trump Plaza opened for business in 1984. But the casino did not make as much money as they had hoped. Compared to other casinos in Atlantic City, including another Harrah's property, Trump's casino came up short.

Trump Plaza, one of three casinos Trump owned in Atlantic City

Trump was not discouraged. Instead, he worked to increase his presence in Atlantic City. He bought a casino property from the hotel company Hilton for $320 million. Trump put his name on this casino as well. It became known as Trump Castle.

Then Holiday Inn became angry that Trump had put his name on another casino that competed with Harrah's. The company sued Trump. He moved quickly and offered to buy out Holiday Inn's half of their partnership. Trump paid Holiday Inn $73 million to gain complete control of Trump Plaza and end the lawsuit.

Next, Trump set his sights on a third casino that

was still under construction. A company called Resorts International was building the Taj Mahal casino. This casino was going to be the world's largest hotel and casino. The project's construction was originally estimated at $185 million, but it grew to more than $500 million. Resorts International offered businesspeople the opportunity to buy shares of the company. The number of shares a person owned would determine if a person had a say in how the company was run. Trump began buying up these shares. He planned to get enough shares so that he could control the company. However, another investor, a television host named Merv Griffin, also had a strong interest in the company. Griffin began buying shares as well. And he offered to pay more for the shares than Trump had been paying.

The Trump Taj Mahal hotel and casino in Atlantic City

Trump waged war against Griffin, calling his actions "futile" and "feeble." The two filed lawsuits against each

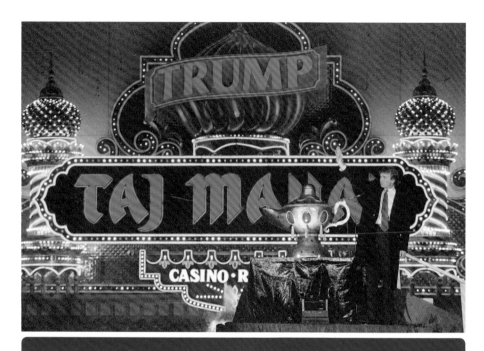

Trump stands at the grand opening of the Trump Taj Mahal casino in 1990.

other, and the media covered the battle. Eventually it became clear that the two investors wanted different things. Trump wanted the Taj Mahal, which was still under construction. Griffin, who was not a real estate developer, wanted to own Resorts International's existing properties. Griffin and Trump finally reached an agreement. Griffin would take control of Resorts International, and then he would sell the Taj Mahal to Trump. When the Trump Taj Mahal opened in 1990, Trump's name was attached to three Atlantic City casinos. This was the maximum number of casinos he was allowed to operate, according to New Jersey laws.

THE ART OF THE DEAL

In 1987 Trump took his business knowledge to the publishing world. With the help of journalist Tony Schwartz, he wrote *Trump: The Art of the Deal*. To gather information for the book, Schwartz followed Trump on the job and listened in as Trump made business deals. The book rocketed to the top of the best-seller lists. Part memoir, part business advice, the book helped make Trump a household name and solidify his image as a clever businessman. Trump also released two more books, *Trump: Surviving at the Top* (1990) and *Trump: The Art of the Comeback* (1997). But he often talks about *The Art of the Deal*. He has said it is the most successful business book ever written. When he announced he would run for president, he said, "We need a leader that wrote *The Art of the Deal*."

Trump signs copies of his 1990 book *Trump: Surviving at the Top*.

LOVE AND LOSS

Although Trump's business was growing and he was reaching new heights of fame, he was about to face some hardship in his personal life. In 1990 Trump's marriage fell apart after Ivana Trump found out that Trump had been spending time with a woman named Marla Maples.

The conflict between Trump and his wife became headline news. He attempted to smooth things over with her, but when Trump left on a trip to Japan, she contacted a divorce lawyer, hired a publicist, and spoke with a gossip columnist. While her husband was halfway around the world, Ivana told her own story to the public.

The couple's bitter divorce played out in the media. Ivana Trump was demanding $1 billion as her share of her husband's fortune. But, as it turned out, Trump didn't have the money. In the end, Ivana agreed to receive $10 million with an additional $650,000 per year in support for herself and her children. However, the very public

Trump and his wife, Ivana, attend a party in New York early in their marriage.

divorce had exposed that Trump's fortune was not as large as many people thought it was. Trump had created an image of himself as a billionaire. But his true wealth was far less than he had let on.

Trump's casinos were performing poorly, and the Trump Organization was losing money. Trump had to declare bankruptcy on all three of his casinos. Some people have criticized Trump for declaring bankruptcy, but Trump sees bankruptcies as a good tool for cutting debts.

Meanwhile, after the divorce, Trump's personal life settled down. He soon announced that he was engaged to Marla Maples. The couple postponed their marriage several times over the next year. Trump insisted on a prenuptial agreement, a contract that says what would happen to each person's money and property if the couple were to get a divorce. Maples did not want to sign it, saying that it would seem to make their marriage less meaningful. Trump insisted. He had built a large business and did not want to go through another messy divorce.

In October 1993, Maples gave birth to their daughter, Tiffany. In December the couple married. But after so much turmoil, the marriage

Trump stands with his wife, Marla Maples, and daughter, Tiffany, in 1995.

was short-lived. In 1997 the couple filed for divorce. Again, the divorce was drawn out in court. But Maples ended up agreeing to the terms of the prenuptial agreement and received $1 million.

It wasn't long before Trump became involved with another woman—a twenty-eight-year-old model named Melania Knauss. In 1998 Trump began attending functions with her. Unlike Ivana Trump, Knauss was uninterested in Trump's business dealings. But she was interested in public success. Perhaps Trump had finally found a match.

Around this time, Trump began to think seriously about running for president. In 1999 Trump joined the Reform Party, a political party that seeks to give Americans another option besides Republican and Democratic Party candidates. The Reform Party wants to change America's trade laws and

Trump poses with Melania Knauss in 1999.

make immigration policies stricter. Trump began a campaign for the party's nomination as a presidential candidate. However, Trump's political ideas were not well

Trump speaks in 1999 during his run for the Reform Party's presidential nomination.

formed. He had few supporters. By February 2000, Trump ended his campaign, saying that the Reform Party was a mess. He had other business avenues to explore instead.

REAL ESTATE TO REALITY TV

In May 2002, the reality television hit *Survivor* filmed its season finale episode in New York. Trump attended the event. In *Survivor* contestants are stranded in a remote location. They live together and complete challenges. One by one, contestants are voted off the island until only one survivor remains. After witnessing the dramatic physical challenges and voting on the show, Trump was impressed. Afterward, he met Mark Burnett, the show's creator and executive producer, and told him that he'd love for them to work together.

With the seed planted, Burnett went home. Although he was busy with *Survivor*, he knew that Trump had star power. He began brainstorming a show that would make the most of Trump's status as a celebrity businessperson. In the show, two teams of job candidates would compete against each other in a contest to win a one-year job contract at the Trump Organization. Trump himself would star in the show and pick the winners, basing his choices on how the candidates performed in a series of challenges.

Trump loved the idea. But he wasn't sure that he would have enough time to star in the show. Burnett offered to film at Trump Tower. He also promised that Trump would be needed on the set for only three or four hours per episode. Satisfied, Trump decided to do the show. He and Burnett agreed to split the profits.

The show, called *The Apprentice*, was set to premiere in January 2004 on NBC. Trump talked up the show, telling the *New York Times*, "I think there's a whole beautiful picture to be painted about business, American business, how beautiful it is, but also how vicious and tough it is." Trump believed he could use the show to teach TV audiences about business.

The show's schedule was grueling for contestants and tested how well they could handle pressure and stress. The first season of *The Apprentice* aired over the course of thirteen weeks, but it was all filmed in one month. The contestants lived and worked together. They performed under tight deadlines to complete whatever challenges the show's producers threw at them. And they also had to prove that they were the most valuable members of their teams.

At the end of each episode, the team that lost the challenge would send its two weakest team members into a boardroom to defend themselves to Trump. Trump sat on the opposite side of the table with two advisers. After listening to the candidates and talking with his advisers, Trump made his decision. One of the candidates would be fired.

Trump (*right*) speaks at a casting call for the second season of *The Apprentice*.

More than twenty million American viewers tuned in to watch the first episode of *The Apprentice*. It quickly became a hit show. Trump's no-nonsense approach and directness with contestants drew admiration. The line he used to dismiss candidates on the show—the blunt "You're fired"—soon became his catchphrase.

CELEBRITY STATUS

Trump used *The Apprentice* and its popularity to promote his brand and his many business endeavors. In his television boardroom, he drank his own brand of bottled water, called Trump Ice. He put his name on many different products too, including fragrances, men's suits, and Visa credit cards. His celebrity status grew, and Trump appeared in commercials. He even hosted an episode of the comedy show *Saturday Night Live*.

During this whirlwind of celebrity, Trump, at the age of fifty-eight, decided to marry Melania Knauss. Trump proposed, giving her a $1.5 million ring. They married on January 22, 2005, in Palm Beach, Florida. The guests included public figures such as Hillary Clinton, Oprah Winfrey, and Shaquille O'Neal. However, Trump's third wedding proved to be a less spectacular event than many had anticipated. Despite his love for self-promotion, Trump refused an offer to broadcast the event on TV. After the wedding, Melania Trump continued to work as a model. The couple had a son, Barron William, in 2006.

Meanwhile, Trump remained a fixture on television with his role on *The Apprentice*. After six seasons, the show's producers decided to rebrand the show in 2008. They cast minor celebrities as contestants. The winner of *The Celebrity Apprentice* would receive a bonus of $250,000 to donate to the charity of the winner's choice.

The celebrity format helped boost ratings, which had slumped over the first couple of seasons. Viewers enjoyed watching the celebrity personalities perform challenges and interact with Trump. Some of the most memorable contestants included musician Bret Michaels, actor Gary Busey, and former NBA player Dennis Rodman.

With a more prominent celebrity status, Trump began to be more vocal about his political opinions. He was

Trump waves during the Conservative Political Action Conference in Washington in 2011.

invited to speak at the Conservative Political Action Conference (CPAC) in 2011. There, Trump spoke about economics and trade. He said that other countries such as China and Mexico had too many economic advantages. Trump believed that America was losing out.

Following his CPAC appearance, Trump became more publicly outspoken about his political ideas. Through his television career, Trump had gained a large following on Twitter. He used Twitter as a platform to share his opinions. He also frequently spoke with hosts of television news shows about his views. Trump criticized former president George W. Bush as well as President Barack Obama, saying that their policies and actions were bad for the country.

TRUMP FOR PRESIDENT

Because Trump had been very outspoken in his criticisms of President Obama, many speculated that the businessman planned to broaden his empire and run for political office. Yet it still took Americans by surprise when Trump announced his candidacy in 2015.

Trump faced immediate backlash after his announcement, in which he said that immigrants can bring problems to the United States. Many people said Trump's comment was racist. They also said that he was creating fear in Americans about the people and economy of the country. Many organizations said they would cut

Trump (*center*) speaks during a debate with other Republican nominees, Ben Carson (*left*) and Ted Cruz (*right*).

their ties with Trump. Two weeks after Trump announced his candidacy, NBC announced that it was ending its relationship with Trump. He would not be returning as the host of *The Celebrity Apprentice*.

Trump did not back down from his comments, and he criticized NBC, saying they didn't understand that the United States had a problem with immigration. He accused NBC of trying to be politically correct. Throughout his campaign, Trump made other controversial statements that some people considered to be offensive. But Trump stood by his statements. He thought it was important to state his views honestly.

"I'm a very smart person," Trump explained. "I could give an answer that's perfect and everything's fine and nobody would care about it, nobody would write about it, or I could give an honest answer, which becomes a big story."

In the Republican primaries, voters responded to his tendency to speak his mind. By May 2016, Trump had secured the Republican nomination. He accepted the nomination in July. He also introduced his running mate, who would become his vice president, Indiana governor Mike Pence.

Then Trump continued his campaign against the Democratic nominee, Hillary Clinton. Again, he did not

Trump debates with Democratic nominee Hillary Clinton on September 26, 2016.

back down from controversy. He criticized Clinton for her involvement in what became known as the e-mail scandal—an incident in which Clinton was accused of deleting government e-mails in an attempt to cover up events surrounding the deaths of four Americans in Benghazi, Libya. The FBI investigated the incident and decided not to press charges against Clinton. But Trump said he wanted to steer the United States away from having someone who'd been involved in such an incident as its leader. He said that typical politicians don't take enough action. He promised that he was the candidate who would be able to make America great again.

Many voters believed in Trump's promise. On November 8, 2016, they took to the polls and made history. Donald Trump was elected to the office of president of the United States. On January 20, 2017, he was officially inaugurated and began his presidency.

Trump quickly got to work to fulfill campaign promises for his first one hundred days in office. He wanted to make changes to immigration laws, trade agreements, and health care. Within the first months of his presidency, Trump signed more than twenty executive orders. He placed bans on individuals entering the United States from several mostly Muslim countries. These bans were blocked by federal judges. Trump also worked to introduce a new health-care plan. However, the plan was dropped when it did not gain enough support from Congress. In January, Trump nominated Judge Neil Gorsuch to the Supreme Court.

FAMILY SUPPORT

Trump's family was very involved and supportive throughout his campaign. Trump and his kids have all said that the family is very close. When the kids were younger, Trump protected them from the media and kept them out of the spotlight. And as they grew up, the three oldest followed Trump into business. They say that they work together, travel together, and go on vacation together. When Trump announced that he would run for president, he said that his family told him that what he was doing would be difficult—but they believed he could do it. Trump's oldest four children, Donald Jr., Ivanka, Eric, and Tiffany, all spoke in support of their father at the Republican National Convention. In his speech, Donald Jr. said that he knew his father could accomplish whatever he set out to do: "I know that when someone tells him that something is impossible, that's what triggers him into action."

Trump stands with his family after announcing his run for president of the United States.

Trump and Pence celebrate as Trump takes to the podium for his acceptance speech on November 9, 2016.

The Senate confirmed this nomination in April 2017.

President Trump continued to use Twitter to post frequently about his actions in office. Throughout his first one hundred days, he and many of his supporters remained positive and hopeful about his success and the future of America.

IMPORTANT DATES

1946 Donald J. Trump is born on June 14 in Queens, New York.

1959 He is enrolled in New York Military Academy.

1968 He graduates from Wharton School with a degree in economics.

1977 He marries Ivana Zelnickova on April 7, with whom he has three children, Donald Jr., Ivanka, and Eric.

1983 Trump Tower opens, bringing Trump national attention.

1984 His first casino, Harrah's at Trump Plaza, opens for business.

1993 He marries Marla Maples on December 20, with whom he has one child, Tiffany.

2004 *The Apprentice* premieres on NBC.

2005 He marries Melania Knauss on January 22, with whom he has one child, Barron William.

2008	*The Celebrity Apprentice* airs on NBC.
2015	He announces his candidacy for president on June 16 at Trump Tower in New York.
2016	He wins the presidential election against Hillary Clinton on November 8.
2017	He is sworn into office and begins his presidency on January 20.

SOURCE NOTES

7 "Here's Donald Trump's Presidential Announcement Speech," *Time*, June 16, 2015, http://time.com/3923128/donald-trump -announcement-speech.

11 Michael D'Antonio, *The Truth about Trump* (New York: St. Martin's Press, 2016), 39.

13 Ibid., 46.

15 Ibid., 55.

22 Ibid., 157.

25 Ibid., 170.

27 "Full Text: Donald Trump Announces a Presidential Bid," *Washington Post*, June 16, 2015, https://www.washingtonpost .com/news/post-politics/wp/2015/06/16/full-text-donald-trump -announces-a-presidential-bid.

32 Abby Ellin, "Business; 'Survivor' Meets Millionaire, and a Show Is Born," *New York Times*, October 19, 2003, http://www .nytimes.com/2003/10/19/business/business-survivor-meets -millionaire-and-a-show-is-born.html.

38 Michael D'Antonio, "With Every Twitch, Gesture and Sneer, Donald Trump Is a Sincere Six Year-Old," *Huffington Post*, November 30, 2015, http://www.huffingtonpost.com/michael-dantonio/ with-every-twitch-gesture_b_8665234.html.

40 Will Drabold, "Watch Donald Trump Jr. Speak at the Republican Convention," *Time*, July 20, 2016, http://time.com/4414200 /republican-convention-donald-trump-jr-speech-transcript -video.

SELECTED BIBLIOGRAPHY

Barron, James. "The Donald Is to Marry! And Darlings, It's Marla!" *New York Times*, July 4, 1991. http://www.nytimes.com/1991/07/04/nyregion/the-donald-is-to-marry-and-darlings-it-s-marla.html.

Blair, Gwenda. *The Trumps: Three Generations of Builders and a Presidential Candidate.* New York: Simon & Schuster, 2015.

D'Antonio, Michael. *Never Enough: Donald Trump and the Pursuit of Success.* New York: Thomas Dunne Books, 2015.

———. *The Truth about Trump.* New York: St. Martin's, 2016.

"Donald Trump Biography." *Biography.com.* Last modified September 23, 2016. http://www.biography.com/people/donald-trump-9511238.

"Donald Trump Biography." *Fox News*, August 2, 2007. http://www.foxnews.com/story/2007/08/02/donald-trump-biography.html.

Ellin, Abby. "Business; 'Survivor' Meets Millionaire, and a Show Is Born." *New York Times*, October 19, 2003. http://www.nytimes.com/2003/10/19/business/business-survivor-meets-millionaire-and-a-show-is-born.html.

Trump, Donald. *The Art of the Deal.* New York: Ballantine Books, 2009.

———. *Great Again: How to Fix Our Crippled America.* New York: Threshold, 2015.

FURTHER READING

BOOKS

Leavitt, Amie Jane. *A History of the Republican Party.* Hockessin, DE: Mitchell Lane, 2013. Read this book to learn about the history of the Republican Party and platforms, as well as notable members of the party.

Maida, Jerome. *Political Power: Donald Trump.* New York: StormFront Entertainment, 2016. Kindle edition. Learn more about Donald Trump's family and how they instilled in him the ambition and energy that has made him a success.

Merberg, Julie, and Sarah Parvis. *How to Start Your Very First Business.* New York: Downtown Bookworks, 2015. Read this book to learn more about business and how you can start pursuing your own business deals.

Sobel, Syl. *Presidential Elections and Other Cool Facts.* Hauppauge, NY: Barron's, 2016. Learn more about politics and how presidential elections work, plus fascinating facts about presidents from George Washington to Barack Obama.

WEBSITES

Donald Trump Biography
http://www.thefamouspeople.com/profiles/donald-trump-3378.php
Take another look at Donald Trump's life and accomplishments, as well as some interesting facts.

Forbes: The World's Billionaires
http://www.forbes.com/profile/donald-trump
Check out Donald Trump's net worth and ranking on *Forbes*'s billionaire's list.

GOP

https://www.gop.com

Read about the Republican Party, its platform, and how to get involved in politics.

President Donald J. Trump

https://www.whitehouse.gov/administration/president-trump

See the official White House page for President Trump.

Trump

http://www.trump.com

Visit the official website of the Trump Organization, and explore Trump's many businesses and projects.

INDEX